Table of Conten

English Language Arts

Mathematics

1

Common Core State Standards

First Grade Workbook
STUDENT EDITION

Grade 1

- ## Math Standards
- ## English Standards

Worksheets that teach every Common Core Standard!

Name: _____

New Friend

Directions: Read, or listen to the teacher read, the passage below about a new friend. Answer the questions about the text. Ask your own question that can be answered by reading the text.

Calliope is my new friend. She is 6 and just moved to our town from Sioux Falls, South Dakota. I have never been to South Dakota. I grew up in Rhode Island. Calliope said that she lived on a farm and had cows and pigs. I only have a dog. I'd love to have a pig! Calliope has 4 brothers, but I am an only child. She also likes country music, but I prefer to listen to Top 40. We are pretty different.

After knowing Calliope for a few weeks, though, I realized that we are a lot alike, too. We both like to read. I have seventeen Barbie dolls, and Calliope has 15! We like to share Barbie clothes. I have a collection of shells I found at the beaches here in Rhode Island and Calliope has a bunch of rocks she collected in the hills of South Dakota. Some even have fossils in them! I think Calliope and I are going to be good friends.

Answer these questions about the text.

1. Who are the main characters?

I and Calliope

2. Where had Calliope lived?

South Dakota

3. How were the two friends different?

top 40 dog pigs cows brothers

4. How were the two friends alike?

pest music read dolls shells

Ask a question about this text.

_____

_____

_____

Level: First Grade   Name: _____

Circus

Directions: Read, or listen to the teacher read, the passage below about a trip to the circus. Answer the questions about the text. Ask your own question that can be answered by reading the text.

   Last week my family and I went to see the circus that came to my town. I was very excited because I had never been to a circus before. Right away the ringmaster introduced the first act. Two acrobats hung from wires high above my head. They did flips and spins and twirls. Next, a small car came out and drove around in circles. When it stopped, clowns began to pile out. I counted them as they climbed out of the tiny car...one, two, three...eight, nine, ten! Wow!

   As the circus went on I saw elephants doing tricks, seals balancing balls on their noses, and a fire-eater! The last act was my favorite. A magician waved his wand and made a lady disappear, and then reappear! It was amazing! I really enjoyed my first circus!

Answer these questions about the text.

1. Where does the story take place?

a Circus

2. Who went to the circus?

I and I's family

3. What were some of the acts at the circus?

Small crs elephants

4. What was the girl's favorite act?

disappedr and reappear

Ask a question about this text.

_____

_____

_____

_____

Standard: Reading I Literature I RL.1.1   ©http://CoreCommonStandards.com

Name: _____

Retelling a Story

Directions: Read a story of your choice, or listen to the teacher read a story to you. Think about what happens at the beginning, middle, and end of the story. What are the important parts in the story? What is the story about and what did you learn?
Draw a picture from the story and retell the story's important parts.

Beginning

Middle

End

Name: _____

The Boy Who Cried Wolf

Directions: Read, or listen to the teacher read, *The Boy Who Cried Wolf.* Retell the story.

The Boy Who Cried Wolf

(handwritten on illustration: I am, a Laier, a dm)

A shepherd-boy, who watched a flock of sheep near a village, was a bit bored and wanted to have some fun. He decided to pretend a wolf was nearby and call for help. "Wolf! Wolf!" the boy cried, and when the villagers came running to help him, he laughed at them for being fooled.

The boy played his trick several times, each time watching and laughing as the villagers came running to help.

The Wolf, however, did truly come at last. The shepherd-boy, now really afraid, shouted in terror: "Pray, do come and help me! The Wolf is killing the sheep!" But no one paid any attention to his cries, and nobody came to help. The Wolf, having no fear and being very hungry, destroyed the whole flock.

Moral: There is no believing a liar, even when he speaks the truth.

Beginning

A shepherd-boy who watched a flock of sheep near a village.

Middle

The boy was a bit bored so he called for herRwolf wolf Theboy cried.

End

Then a rEAL WOlf came by the boy cried for help but nobody came.

©http://CoreCommonStandards.com

Name: _____

Telling About the Story

Directions: Read, or listen to the teacher read, a story you know. Retell the story by filling in the parrot's speech bubbles.

Book Title _____

Who Are the Main Characters?

Where Does the Story Take Place?

What's the Problem

What is the Solution?

Standard: Reading I Literature I RL.1.3

Level: First Grade   Name: _____

Important Parts of the Story

Directions: Read, or listen to the teacher read, a story. Draw a picture and write important details about the characters, setting, and events from the story.

_____
Book Title

Who Are the Main Characters?

Where Does the Story Take Place?

Important Event

Important Event

Name: _____

Finding Feelings

Directions: Read the short story below. Write the words that express feelings or make you feel a certain way when you read them.

I went to the circus last night with my family. I was very excited. The clowns were very funny and made me happy to watch them. I was nervous when I saw the acrobats hanging high above us. My tummy was growling so mom bought me some popcorn. When the elephants came out all in a line, one stumbled and we all gasped. I felt sorry that the elephant tripped. My sister started to cry. But I hugged her and told her the elephant was just fine and she'd enjoy watching his tricks. My sister smiled and I knew she was happy again. The rest of the circus was fun and we had a great time. I can't wait until the circus comes back to town!

These are words I see above that show feelings.

_____   _____
_____   _____
_____   _____
_____   _____
_____   _____

These are words I see above that make me feel...

These words...   make me feel...

_____   _____
_____   _____
_____   _____
_____   _____

Standard: Reading I Literature I RL.1.4

©http://CoreCommonStandards.com

Level: First Grade   Name: _____

Finding Feelings

Directions: Choose a story to read with a partner from your classroom library. You may see some words that tell how the characters feel. You may see words that make you feel a certain way. Write the words that express feelings or make you feel a certain way when you read them.

The story we read: _____

These are words I see that show feelings.

These are words I see that make me feel...

These words...   make me feel...

Name: _____

Story or Information?

Directions: Look at the book covers below. If possible, read both books. Compare the two books about wasps. How are they alike? How are they different?

This book is

☐ non-fiction
☐ fiction

Does this story have characters?

yes   no

Does this story have a setting?

yes   no

Does this story have a problem?

yes   no

What is the purpose of this story?

entertain

persuade

inform

This book is

☐ non-fiction
☐ fiction

Does this story have characters?

yes   no

Does this story have a setting?

yes   no

Does this story have a problem?

yes   no

What is the purpose of this story?

entertain

persuade

inform

Name: _____

Story or Information?

Directions: Choose two books; one that is a story, one that gives information about something. If possible, read both books. Compare the two books. How are they alike? How are they different?

_____ Title of Book One How does this book look different than the other? Think about the pictures and how the text is written. Does it have... ☐ headings? ☐ chapters? ☐ diagrams? ☐ illustrations? ☐ glossary? ☐ table of contents? ☐ captions?	Does this story have characters? *yes no* Does this story have a setting? *yes no* Does this story have a problem? *yes no* What is the purpose of this story? *entertain* *persuade* *inform*
_____ Title of Book Two How does this book look different than the other? Think about the pictures and how the text is written. Does it have... ☐ headings? ☐ chapters? ☐ diagrams? ☐ illustrations? ☐ glossary? ☐ table of contents? ☐ captions?	Does this story have characters? *yes no* Does this story have a setting? *yes no* Does this story have a problem? *yes no* What is the purpose of this story? *entertain* *persuade* *inform*

Standard: Reading I Literature I RL.1.5   ©http://CoreCommonStandards.com

Name: _____

What Kind of Story?

Directions: With your teacher's help, match the book cover to the type of story it is. (genre)

poem

story

fantasy

non-fiction

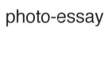

photo-essay

mythology

history

realistic fiction

play

mystery

fable

fairy tale

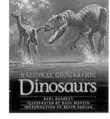

Standard: Reading I Literature I RL.1.5

©http://CoreCommonStandards.com

Name: _____

Who's Talking Now?

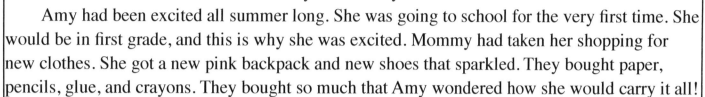

Directions: Read the short story below.
Write which character is telling the story by reading the words below.

Amy Goes to First Grade
By: Deborah Lynn

Amy had been excited all summer long. She was going to school for the very first time. She would be in first grade, and this is why she was excited. Mommy had taken her shopping for new clothes. She got a new pink backpack and new shoes that sparkled. They bought paper, pencils, glue, and crayons. They bought so much that Amy wondered how she would carry it all!

Then, when it was time to go to school, Amy felt butterflies in her tummy. She felt afraid.

"What if the kids will not play with me? What if the teacher is mean?" she wondered. Amy was afraid the teacher would ask her things she would not know how to answer. Amy's mother said all the kids have feelings like this when they go to school for the first time.

"When you go to school you will really like it. You will meet lots of new friends and learn many new things," her mom told her. "When you get to school, find another little girl who looks scared, and try to help her to feel better. If you do that," her mother said, "you will feel happy because you helped someone else."

This is just what Amy did. When her mother dropped her off at school and she felt all alone, she looked around and found another little girl who felt the same way. They became friends. Amy found out that she loved school. She loved her teacher and she loved to learn new things!

Who is telling the story?

Who said? "What if the kids will not play with me? What if the teacher is mean?"

_____

Who said? "When you go to school you will really like it."

_____

Who said? "When you get to school, find another little girl who looks scared, and try to help her to feel better."

_____

Who said? Amy had been excited all summer long.

_____

Name: _____

Who's Talking?

Directions: Read the short story below.
Write which character is telling the story by reading the words below.

A Fall Festival with Grandma
By: Deborah Lynn

It would soon be Halloween and Mommy and Daddy wanted their kids to have fun!

"What can we do so that Eva and Micah will be safe?" asked Mommy.

"Let them go to the Fall Festival with Grandma. That would be lots of fun!" Daddy answered.

"Yes Mommy, please," Eva begged. "Let us go to the Fall Festival."

"What is a Fall Festival?" Micah asked. Mommy explained that it was a place where the people from Grandma's church would have games and prizes. She said they would like it very much. There would be many children there. So when Halloween arrived, Grandma came over to get Eva and Micah. Eva was dressed up as a Princess and Micah looked like Spiderman. "This is going to be way cool!" Micah said with a smile.

The festival was outside at a football field. They had bounce houses, walls to climb and swings that went around and around and way up high. There were pony rides, a petting zoo and lots of games to play. Everyone at the festival won candy even if they didn't win the game! There were hot dogs, drinks, pretzels and cotton candy. There was so much to do that they didn't have time to do it all.

They stayed until the rides closed and then they walked back to the car in the dark. It really was a very fun night, and on the way home Grandma even stopped at the ice cream store. Eva and Micah got two scoops of chocolate ice cream.

"I had fun Grandma," Micah said.

"Me too, Grandma, thanks for taking us," Eva said. Grandma just smiled. I think she was happy too.

Who is telling the story?

Who said? "Let them go to the Fall Festival with Grandma. That would be lots of fun!"

_____

Who said? "This is going to be way cool!"

_____

Who said? There were pony rides, a petting zoo and lots of games to play.

_____

Who said? "Me too, Grandma, thanks for taking us."

_____

Name: _____

Character and Settings

Directions: After reading a story of your choice, describe a character and the setting by using details from the story.

Story Title: _____

Draw a picture of one of the main characters.
Describe the character by using details from the story.

_____
_____
_____
_____
_____

Draw a picture of the setting from the story.
Describe the setting by using details from the story.

_____
_____
_____
_____
_____

Name: _____

Important Events

Directions: After reading a story of your choice, describe two events using details from the story.

Story Title: _____

Draw a picture of one of the important events.
Describe the event by using details from the story.

Draw a picture of another important events.
Describe the event by using details from the story.

Level: First Grade

Name: _____

Frog & Toad Together

Directions: Read *Frog and Toad Together*. Compare and contrast the adventures the two characters have in the book.

What happens to Frog and Toad in *The Garden*?

What happens to Frog and Toad in *Cookies*?

What happens to Frog and Toad in *The Dream*?

How are Frog and Toad alike?

How are Frog and Toad different?

Level: First Grade   Name: _____

Green Eggs and Ham

Directions: Read *Green Eggs and Ham*. Compare and contrast the two characters,
Sam-I-Am and Sam's friend. Describe the characters and what they
do in the story.

What are some words that would describe Sam-I-Am?

What are some of the things Sam-I-Am does during the story?

What are some words that would describe Sam-I-Am's friend?

What are some of the things Sam-I-Am's friend does during the story?

Why do you think Sam-I-Am is trying to get his friend to try green eggs and ham?

Why do you think Sam-I-Am's friend finally tries the green eggs and ham?

Would you?

Standard: Reading I Literature I RL.1.9
Graphics (c) www.birthdayexpress.com

©http://CoreCommonStandards.com

Level: First Grade   Name: _____

What I Am Reading

Directions: Keep track of the stories you read this year in First Grade. When you finish a book, write the title and the date you completed the book. Did you like the book?

Date	Book Title	Did You Like the Book?

Standard: Reading I Literature I RL.1.10

Name: _____

What Are They Reading?

Directions: Keep track of the stories your students can read this year at grade level. Write the date each genre was read successfully.

Name	non-fiction story	realistic fiction story	fantasy story	informational story	poetry

Standard: Reading I Literature I RL.1.10

Name: _____

Ferrets

Directions: Read, or listen to the teacher read, the passage below about ferrets. Answer the questions about the text. Ask your own question that can be answered by reading the text.

      I just got a new pet. It is a ferret. A ferret is a mammal. The name ferret means "thief" and it is a good name for this animal because it likes to steal things in the house and hide them. My mom's car keys were missing and so was my brother's toy truck. We found both of them inside dad's chair, along with a pen, a necklace, and my sock.

      Ferrets are mostly brown but can have silver, black, and white fur as well. They are long, thin animals and are very playful. They like to sleep long hours each day, but when they are awake they climb, roll, and run around. I feed my ferret pellets made of meat, because a ferret is a carnivore and must have meat to eat.

      Ferrets have long nails and sharp teeth, but because I take care of my ferret, he is friendly and lovable. My ferret will make a great pet.

Answer these questions about the text.

1. What kind of animal is a ferret?

_____

2. What do ferrets like to do?

_____

3. Why do you need to feed a ferret meat?

_____

4. Why would a ferret make a good pet?

_____

Ask a question about this text.

_____

_____

Name: _____

Pillbugs

Directions: Read, or listen to the teacher read, the passage below about pillbugs. Answer the questions about the text. Ask your own question that can be answered by reading the text.

My class is studying pillbugs this month. I used to be afraid to touch anything with a lot of legs, but now, I think they are cool. I always thought that pillbugs were insects, but they are not. They are actually crustaceans, like a lobster! Pillbugs have 14 legs, not six like an insect. And, like fish, pillbugs breathe through gills, but, they don't live in water. As pillbugs grow, they shed their skin and when they are afraid, well, in danger, they curl up like a ball, or a pill. They are sometimes called roly-polies since they do this.

Pillbugs are tiny. They only grow to about 1/2 inch long. Maybe this is because they eat things that are dead plants. You can find them a lot when you lift a rotten log. They like the dark, moist, dead places.

I like to hold pillbugs because they don't bite and their little feet tickle. I hope to learn more about pillbugs.

Answer these questions about the text.

1. What kind of animal is a pillbug?

_____

2. How many legs does a pillbug have?

_____

3. What do pillbugs eat?

_____

4. Why do pillbugs like to live under rotting logs?

_____

Ask a question about this text.

_____

_____

_____

Name: _____

Earthworms

Directions: Read the passage below about earthworms. What is the main topic of the text? Write some details about the topic. Ask *who, what, where, when, how, why?*

Earthworms are animals found in soil. They have no legs or backbones, and are called invertebrates. Their bodies are soft and can be brown, pink, or even red. Earthworms have a brain and 5 hearts. They do not have lungs. Earthworms eat soil and plant matter as they burrow down into the soil. These tunnels let water and air find ways into the earth to get to the roots of plants. The soil that the earthworms eat passes through their bodies and is left in little piles on the ground. Farmers like to use these *castings* as fertilizer for their gardens. Earthworms help make the soil healthy.

detail	detail

_____
main topic

detail	detail

©http://CoreCommonStandards.com

Level: First Grade   Name: _____

Whales

Directions: Read the passage below about whales. What is the main topic of the text? Write some details about the topic. Ask *who, what, where, when, how, why?*

Whales are animals that live in the ocean. Whales are mammals because they are born alive and drink milk from their mothers when they are young. Whales have lungs and breathe air. But, whales have a blowhole instead of a nose. There are two types of whales; baleen and toothed. Baleen whales have brush-like mouths and eat krill. All toothed-whales eat fish and some eat seals. The blue whale is the largest animal on the earth. People can see whales on a whale watch trip.

detail	detail

_____   main topic

detail	detail

Level: First Grade   Name: _____

Thinking About Characters

Directions: After reading a story and discussing its characters, draw a picture of two of the characters below. Write one attribute that makes each character different from the other, and write one way each character is alike.

Character name _____   **Character name** _____

How this character is different: _____   **How this character is different:** _____

_____   _____

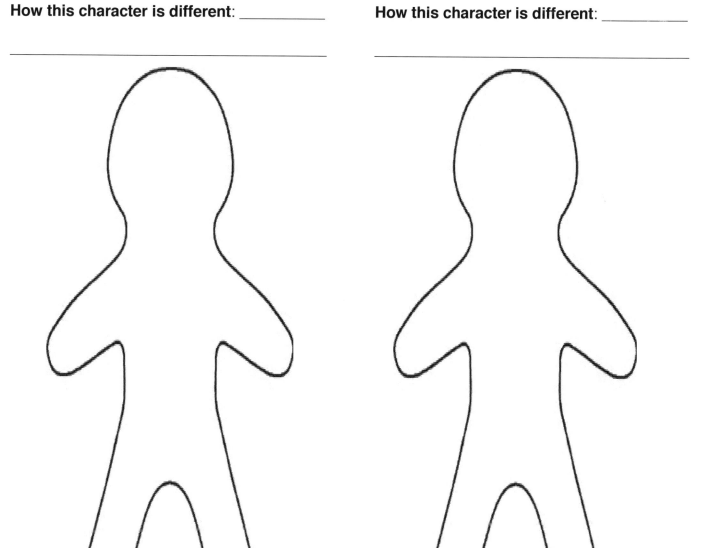

How the characters are the same: _____

_____

Standard: Reading I Informational Text I RI.1.3   ©http://CoreCommonStandards.com

Level: First Grade

Comparing Events

Name: _____

Directions: Listen to an informational story and compare two events. How are they alike? How are they different?

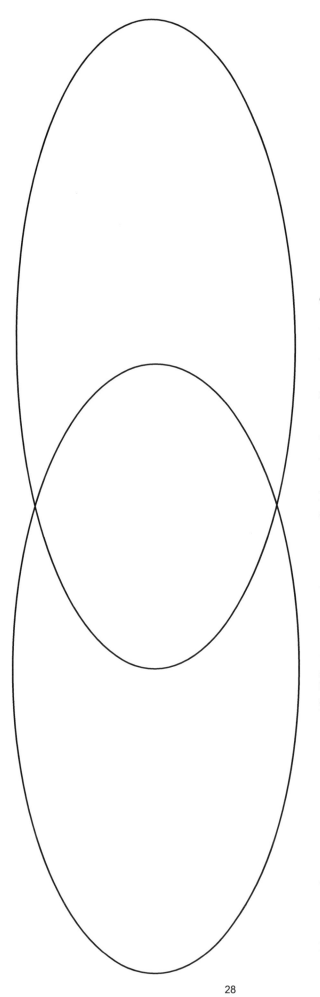

How are the two events connected? What causes the events? How do they affect the story?

_____

_____

_____

_____

28

Standard: Reading I Informational Text I RI.1.3

Name: _____

Understanding Meaning

Directions: Sometimes, even though we can read a word, we may not know what the word means. We can use clues and ask questions to help us understand what the word means.

Penguins

Penguins are black and white birds that do not fly. They are shaped like a **torpedo** which makes them great swimmers. Penguins are **warm-blooded**, like people, but they live in a very cold place; **Antarctica**. They stay warm because under their skin they have layers of fat called **blubber**. Penguins have feathers that also help to keep them dry. But, on really cold days, a group of penguins **huddles** together to stay warm.

Choose a word from the passage. What clues do you see that help you understand what the word means? What can you ask to help you better understand what the word means?

huddles: *words that help me...group, together, warm*

If my friends and I were outside in the wind and cold, what would we do to stay warm?

Now, you read the passage and get the meaning.

Cactus

A cactus is a plant that grows in places that are arid, or have very little water. Deserts grow many different kinds of cacti. A cactus is able to hold onto its water because its leaves are tiny. They are actually needles. Most plants have large leaves and lose water to the air. A cactus' tiny needles lose less water to the air. A cactus has a green stem to make its own food. This is called photosynthesis. Since the leaves are so small, they cannot make the food like most other leaves do. The tallest cactus in the world is 67 feet high. Some of the oldest cacti are 250 years old.

Here is a word I don't know: _____

Words that help me understand: _____

_____

Here are some questions I asked: _____

_____

_____

_____

Standard: Reading I Informational Text I RI.1.4   ©http://CoreCommonStandards.com
Graphic (c) www.telegraph.co.uk

Name: _____

The Venus Fly Trap

Directions: Read the short story below. Are there any words you do not know? Write the words in the box below. Work with a partner to ask questions that may help you better understand the meanings of words.

The Venus Fly Trap

Most plants make their own food. This is called photosynthesis. But the Venus Fly Trap eats meat! Bugs, to be exact. It's a carnivore. It eats animals like spiders, flies, caterpillars, and crickets.   The Venus Fly Trap grows in North Carolina and South Carolina in swampy bogs. This is why it needs to eat insects and arachnids. The soil where Venus Fly Traps grow doesn't have everything the plants need to make their own food. So, they have to eat things like slugs and dragonflies to have what they need to grow.

You can have your own Venus Fly Trap. Just make sure to feed it every day.

These are some words I do not know.

_____   _____

_____   _____

_____   _____

_____   _____

_____   _____

Here are some questions I asked.

_____

_____

_____

_____

_____

Standard: Reading I Informational Text I RI.1.4

©http://CoreCommonStandards.com

Graphic (c) www.telegraph.co.uk

Name: _____

Nonfiction Text Features

Information books are **nonfiction**. They are about things that are true.
Directions: Answer the questions about the Table of Contents and Index.

Table of Contents

	page
seeds	5
stems	9
leaves	12
flowers	16
trees	21

1. What do you think this book is about?

_____

2. Write page numbers for these topics:

leaves _____   flowers _____   seeds _____

trees _____   stems _____

3. What page would you find information about trees?

Page _____

Index

bees	6, 8	seeds	5, 6, 17
petals	16	stamen	16, 17
roots	7, 17, 22	wind	6, 7

4. On which pages would you find these words?

bees _____   petals _____   roots _____

seeds _____   stamen _____ wind _____

5. Can you read about wind on page 16? _____

6. Are the words in alphabetical order? _____

Standard: Reading I Informational Text I RI.1.5   ©http://CoreCommonStandards.com

Name: _____

Nonfiction Text Features

Information books are **nonfiction**. They are about things that are true.

Directions: Choose different nonfiction books to look at. Find examples of the following nonfiction text features. Find examples and write them in the Example column.

FEATURE	WHAT IS IT?	EXAMPLE
Drawings	Drawings of something that fits in the story. Not a real picture.	
Diagrams	A drawing or photo with labeled parts.	
Photographs	Real life pictures of something that fits the story.	
Captions	Words in small print under a photo or diagram. They are often in small print or even in *italics*.	
Headings	The title of a section of a story. Often this is in **Bold** or CAPITALIZED.	
Glossary	A dictionary for the book showing key words and definitions. It may include pronunciation keys, too.	
Index	The index is a listing of what is in a book or story and the page numbers each thing can be found on. It is usually in the back of the book.	
Vocabulary	Important and new words in a story might be **Bold**, Underlined, Highlighted, or in *Italics*.	

Standard: Reading I Informational Text I RI.1.5

Name: _____

Text or Picture?

Directions: Read the text below about elephants. Answer the questions. Circle if you found the information by reading the text or looking at the picture.

The African elephant is very big! It is the biggest land animal on Earth. It is also one of the smartest land animals. The elephant has a long trunk and two white tusks.

Elephants live in Africa and can live for up to 60 years of age. They love to eat and drink. In fact, elephants spend half of the day eating. Their favorite foods are grass, twigs, and fruit.

1. Where do elephants live? _____   **text or picture ?**

2. What color is an elephant? _____   **text or picture ?**

3. Are elephants small or big? _____   **text or picture ?**

4. How old can an elephant live to be? _____   **text or picture ?**

5. Do elephants have pointy ears? _____   **text or picture ?**

6. Is an elephant smart? _____   **text or picture ?**

7. What does an elephant eat? _____   **text or picture ?**

8. How many legs does an elephant have? _____   **text or picture ?**

Name: _____

Text or Picture?

Directions: Read the text below about lions. Write information you learned by reading the text or looking at the pictures.

The lion is the king of the jungle. They are big and strong. Lions weigh 400 pounds and stand 4 feet tall. If you feel the hair on its face, it is soft.

You can find a lion in Africa. They can live for 15 years in the wild. They like to sleep in the grass at night. Lions eat meat, such as zebras, giraffe, and buffalo. Lions live in groups, called "prides", with about 15 other lions.

Write 5 pieces of information you learned by reading the text.
_____
_____
_____
_____
_____
_____
_____
_____
_____
_____
_____

Write 5 pieces of information you learned by looking at the picture.
_____
_____
_____
_____
_____
_____
_____
_____
_____
_____

Standard: Reading I Informational Text I RI.1.6

Name: _____

Key Ideas: Butterflies

Directions: Read the text below about butterflies. Write information you learned by reading the text or looking at the pictures.

    The butterfly is a flying insect with two wings and two antennae. They have three main body parts: the head, thorax and abdomen. Butterflies have a long proboscis, or tongue, that they use to drink nectar from plants.

    Butterflies come in many different colors and sizes.   Butterflies live only around 40 days.   Some butterflies only live for three to four days.

    A butterfly starts out as an egg and grows into a caterpillar. The caterpillar then forms a chrysalis. Inside of the chrysalis, the caterpillar turns into a butterfly.

    You can find butterflies anywhere in the world, except for Antarctica.

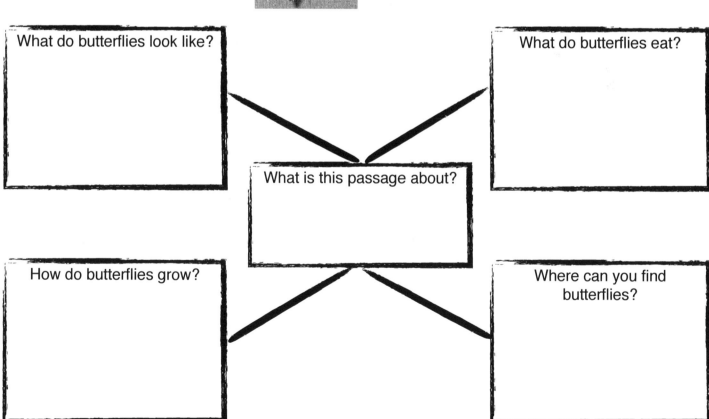

What do butterflies look like?

What do butterflies eat?

What is this passage about?

How do butterflies grow?

Where can you find butterflies?

©http://CoreCommonStandards.com

Name: _____

Key Ideas: Manatees

Directions: Read the text below about manatees. Write information you learned by reading the text or looking at the pictures.

The Florida manatee is a big animal that lives in the warm water. Some people say that it looks like a cow. They have flippers and a tail to help them swim.

Manatees only eat plants. These gentle, friendly animals can swim in the water, but they need to stick their nose out of the water to breathe. That is because the manatee is a mammal.

These large mammals are endangered. That means that there are not many manatees left on Earth. Manatees often get hurt by boat propellers. Many people are working hard to save the manatee from extinction.

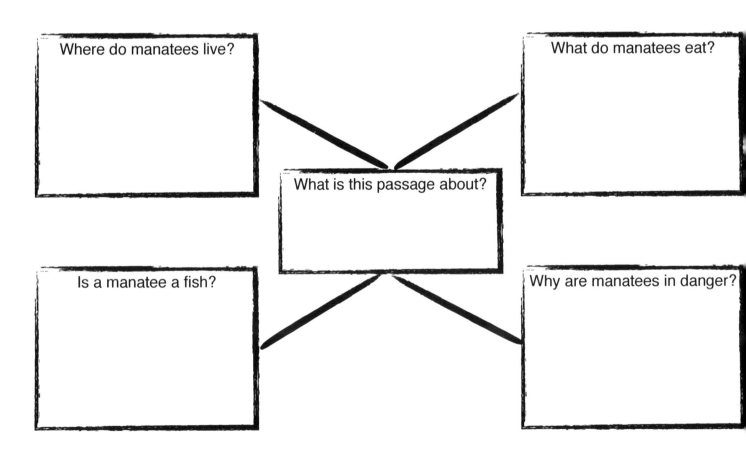

Where do manatees live?

What do manatees eat?

What is this passage about?

Is a manatee a fish?

Why are manatees in danger?

Level: First Grade

Name: ______________________________

Making a Point

Directions: Read an informational piece of text. What is the main point the author is trying to get across? What are the reasons the author gives to support his point? Complete the chart below.

The text I chose is ______________________________

Written by ______________________________

The author is trying to tell us that ______________________________

____

____

Here are some reasons in the text that help me see the author's point.

Standard: Reading I Informational Text I RI.1.8

Name: _____

Supporting the Point

Directions: Read the passage below about ice cream. What are the reasons the author gives for ice cream being healthy?

Ice Cream MUST Be Healthy!

We should eat ice cream every day! It is the healthiest food on the planet! My mother disagrees with me. But I know I am right.

Ice cream is made from milk. Milk has calcium. Mom says I should drink milk every day. So, I think I should eat ice cream every day.   I like strawberry ice cream the best! Strawberries are a fruit! Fruit is healthy! So strawberry ice cream must be heathy, too!

My teacher said that nuts are in the meat food group. I like nuts on my ice cream. So, it's like I am eating meat. Meat has protein. And protein is good for you!

Finally, whenever I eat ice cream, I get really thirsty and always want a big glass of water. Water is a very healthy drink. My doctor says I should drink lots of water. If I eat lots of ice cream, I'll want lots of water!

I think ice cream is the healthiest food on the planet!

What reasons in the text does the author give to support ice cream being healthy?

Name: _____

Comparing Similar Texts: illustrations

Directions: After reading two different stories about the same topic, complete the chart to identify similarities and differences between the illustrations.

Titles		
Topic		
Illustrations How are the illustrations similar? What types of illustrations are used? What information do they help to explain?		
Illustrations How are the illustrations different? Does one piece have more, or less? Do the illustrations explain different ideas? What types of illustrations are used? Photographs? Drawings? Paintings? diagrams?		

39

Standard: Reading I Informational Text I RI.1.9

Name: _____

Comparing Similar Texts: organizing data

Directions: After reading two different stories about the same topic, complete the chart to identify similarities and differences between how data is organized.

Titles		
Topic		
Organization How is the information organization similar? What does the information show? Is it displayed as a graph? Checklist? Bold type? In chapters? As diagrams?		
Organization How is the information organization different? What does the information show? Is it displayed as a graph? Checklist? Bold type? In chapters? As diagrams?		

Standard: Reading I Informational Text I RI.1.9

Level: First Grade   Name: _____

Nonfiction I Am Reading

Directions: Keep track of the nonfiction text you read this year in First Grade. When you finish a book, write the title and the date you completed the book. What was the topic?

Date	Book Title	Topic

Standard: Reading I Informational Text I RI.1.10   ©http://CoreCommonStandards.com

Name: _____

What Are They Reading?

Directions: Keep track of the nonfiction text your students can read this year at grade level. Write the date each type of text was read successfully.

Name	nonfiction storybook	photo-graphic essay	auto-biography	informational book	journal/ diary

Standard: Reading I Informational Text I RI.1.10

Name: _____

I Can Read

Directions: Read the sentences below. Start at the left and move to the right. Follow the directions.

Bob runs over the grass to get the ball.

Underline the FIRST word of the sentence.

Circle the PERIOD in the sentence.

LuLu likes to fly her kite in the park.

Underline the CAPITAL LETTER at the beginning of the sentence.

Circle the PERIOD in the sentence.

Directions: Correct the sentences below.

frogs sit on pads in the lake

_____

_____

i can run and kick the rock in my yard

_____

_____

my mom hugs me at night before bed

_____

_____

Name: _____

I Can Read

Directions: Read the sentences below. Start at the left and move to the right.
Follow the directions.

Jack sees the boat and wants to go for a ride.

Underline the FIRST word of the sentence.

Circle the PERIOD in the sentence.

Little Bear plays with his sister in the pool.

Underline the CAPITAL LETTER at the beginning of the sentence.

Circle the PERIOD in the sentence.

Directions: Write the words below correctly into a sentence. Don't forget to use a capital letter
and a period.

play my likes mouse with the cat to

_____

- -

_____

fly bird tree to the can this

_____

- -

_____

jump snowballs in make the snow and we

_____

- -

_____

Name: _____

I Can Read These Words

Directions: Look at the words below. They are all one-syllable words made of three sounds. Read the words. Listen to the sounds you hear.
Think about the sounds each letter or blend makes. Complete the words.

word	phonemes	picture
cat	c-a-t	
flip	fl-i-p	
stop	_ _ - _ - _	
frog	_ _ - _ - _	
fist	_ - _ - _ _	
sled	_ _ - _ - _	

Standard: Reading I Foundational Skills I RF.1.2   ©http://CoreCommonStandards.com

Find the Phonemes: blends

Directions: Look at the words below. Each word has three sounds, but may have more than three letters. Sometimes letters work together to make one sound. The sounds you hear in the words are called phonemes. Write the phonemes properly into the Elkonin Boxes below.

dr	u	m

drum

plop

tent

slip

chimp

bat

stink

lost

Level: First Grade   Name: _____

Find the Phonemes: digraphs

Directions: Look at the words below. Each word has three sounds, but may have more than three letters. Sometimes letters work together to make one sound. The sounds you hear in the words are called phonemes. Write the phonemes properly into the Elkonin Boxes below.

ch	i	ck

chick

shut

push

that

duck

math

king

chop

Standard: Reading I Foundational Skills I RF.1.3   ©http://CoreCommonStandards.com

47

Name: _____

Counting Syllables

Directions: Some words have one syllable. Some words have more than one syllable. Each syllable needs a vowel sound. Fill in the missing vowels and write the number of syllables in each word.

1. **chick___n**

There are _____ syllables in this word.

2. **art___st**

There are _____ syllables in this word.

3. **n___st**

There are _____ syllables in this word.

4. **w___men**

There are _____ syllables in this word.

5. **f___nger**

There are _____ syllables in this word.

6. **p___ttern**

There are _____ syllables in this word.

7. **lumb___r**

There are _____ syllables in this word.

8. **d___ffer___nt**

There are _____ syllables in this word.

Level: First Grade   Name: _____

Reading With Fluency

nonfiction

Directions: When you read, you are not just saying the words. Readers read with a purpose and to understand. Practice reading orally so that you can be a fluent reader.

Read the passage below while your teacher times you. Try to read as many words accurately as you can in one minute. Try again in a couple of weeks to see if your fluency improves. {Goal of 80 WPM}

The Bottlenose Dolphin

Bottlenose dolphins are some of the smartest mammals in the ocean! They swim in groups and talk to each other by squeaking and whistling. Most grow to be 8 to 12 feet long and can live for 50 years.

Bottlenose dolphins come to the top of the water to breathe every 2 or 3 minutes, but they can hold their breath much longer. They breathe out a hole on top of their heads called a blowhole. They eat fish and squid, but they do not chew their food. They prefer to swallow it whole!

Date	Words Read Correctly Per Minute

Standard: Reading I Foundational Skills I RF.1.4   ©http://CoreCommonStandards.com

Name: _____

Reading With Fluency

fiction

Directions: When you read, you are not just saying the words. Readers read with a purpose and to understand. Practice reading orally so that you can be a fluent reader.

Read the passage below while your teacher times you. Try to read as many words accurately as you can in one minute. Try again in a couple of weeks to see if your fluency improves.

New Crayons

Billy likes to color. He got new crayons.

He does not know the right colors. He makes things fun!

He draws purple apples. He draws green clouds.

He draws blue monkeys. He draws orange lakes.

He draws pink dogs. He draws grey bananas.

He makes yellow car tires. He makes black suns.

He likes to draw brown rain.

He likes to draw red rabbits.

Billy does not know his colors. Billy makes fun things.

Date	Words Read Correctly Per Minute

Name: _____

My Opinion

Directions: Read or listen to *The Big Orange Splot* by Daniel Manus Pinkwater. Do you agree with what Mr. Plumbean did to his house? Do you think he was right, or were the neighbors right? Write your opinion and use text evidence to support your reasons.

_____

_____

_____

_____

_____

_____

_____

_____

_____

_____

_____

_____

_____

_____

_____

_____

_____

_____

_____

_____

_____

_____

_____

_____

_____

_____

_____

_____

Name: _____

An Interesting Person

Directions: Choose an interesting person from a story that you are reading in class. Write about that person and why you think he or she is interesting. Use words from the text to support your opinions. Draw a picture of the person.

Name: _____

<u>Just the Facts</u>

Directions: Choose a topic that interests you or that you are discussing in class. Write an informative text piece that names the topic, gives facts about the topic, and ends so the reader feels the writing is complete.

Name: _____

Animal Facts

Directions: Choose an animal that interests you or that you are discussing in class. Write an informative text piece that names the animal, gives facts about the animal, and ends so the reader feels the writing is complete.

Name: _____

Lesson Learned

Directions: Fables teach us lessons. Think of a time when you learned a lesson. Write a story about a time that you learned a lesson. State the lesson and give details about what happened. Make sure you have proper sequence in your story and that it has a beginning, middle, and end.

Standard: Reading I Writing I W.1.3

Name: _____

Creative

Directions: Think of a time when you created something. Write a story about a time that you created an art project, sculpture, model, or even food. Provide detail about what you created. Make sure you have proper sequence in your story and that it has a beginning, middle, and end.

Name: _____

Work In Progress

Directions: Write about something that you like to do. Share your writing with a friend. Listen to questions and suggestions your friend has and work together to make your writing better. Edit your writing to correct spelling, punctuation, and grammar.

_____

Level: First Grade   Name: _____

Work In Progress

Directions: Write a short story about the picture below. Share your writing with a friend. Listen to questions and suggestions your friend has and work together to make your writing better. Edit your writing to correct spelling, punctuation, and grammar.

_____
- -
_____
- -
_____
- -
_____
- -
_____
- -
_____
- -
_____
- -
_____
- -
_____
- -
_____
- -
_____
- -
_____
- -
_____

Name: _____

Other Ways to Write

Directions: Today, many people use digital tools to write. Write your story using the computer and other digital tools.

My topic is...

_____

_____

I am going to use a computer to create my story.

I want to add pictures to my story by using...

a. *digital camera*, b. *scanner*, c. *clipart website*.

I will share my writing by...

a. *printing my story*,
b. *emailing it to my classmates*,
c. *presenting it using a projector*

Something new I learned using these tools is...

_____

_____

_____

_____

Standard: Reading I Writing I W.1.6
Graphics (c) ScrappinDoodles

Name: _____

Using Digital Resources

Directions: Today, many people use digital tools to write. Use this checklist to record what digital skills each student can perform.

Digital Skill	Date	Success
Can turn on a computer.		
Can shut down a computer.		
Uses a mouse well. (Can double-click; move cursor to desired place; scroll if available.)		
Knows where most common characters are on keyboard.		
Can log in and out of programs.		
Can change the font or size of font.		
Knows how to use space bar; back space; delete; and return.		
Can add a graphic.		
Can drag and drop an item.		
Can copy/paste an item.		
Can save a file.		
Can print work.		
Can click through a Powerpoint Presentation		

Standard: Reading I Writing I W.1.6

©http://CoreCommonStandards.com

Name: _____

Research Together

Directions: Work with a partner, or a group, to research a topic using "How-to" books. Write a sequence of instructions to explain your topic.

How To

_____

First _____

_____

Second _____

_____

Third _____

_____

Fourth _____

_____

Fifth _____

Standard: Reading I Writing I W.1.7
Graphics (c) ScrappinDoodles

Name: _____

How To

Directions: Work with a partner to write a series of steps that teach someone how to do a particular task. Use pictures, labels, and sentences to express your ideas. Act the steps out to be sure your ideas follow the correct order. Use enough detail.

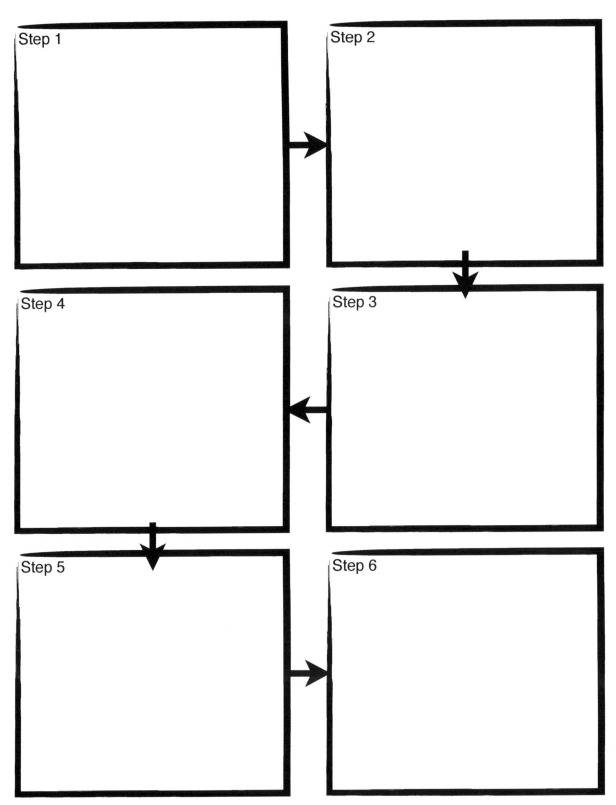

Step 1

Step 2

Step 4

Step 3

Step 5

Step 6

Standard: Reading I Writing I W.1.7

Name: _____

Experience Narrative

Directions: Think about a time in your life you want to tell about. Think about where you were, who you were with, what you did, and how you felt. Write a story and provide detail that will help the reader relive the experience with you.

_____

Name: _____

Answering a Question

Directions: You have a question to answer. Think about the question. Use resources your teacher provides to find information to help you answer the question. Write your answer below.

```
┌ ─ ─ ─ ─ ─ ─ ─ ─ ─ ─ ─ ─ ─ ─ ─ ─ ┐
|                                  |
|          paste question here     |
|                                  |
└ ─ ─ ─ ─ ─ ─ ─ ─ ─ ─ ─ ─ ─ ─ ─ ─ ┘
```

I am using resources my teacher gave me.
This is some information I found to help me answer the question.

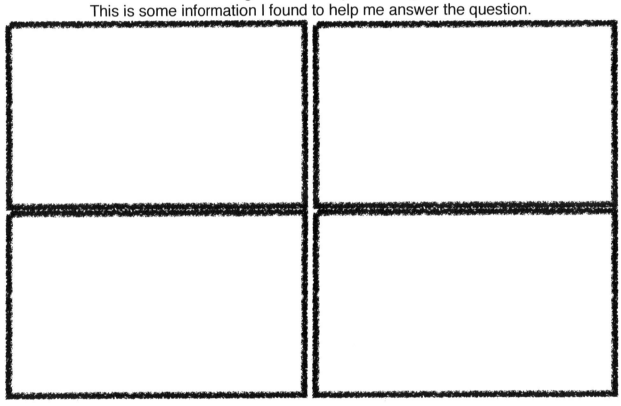

Here is my answer to the question and why I think I am right.

_____
_____
_____
_____
_____
_____
_____
_____
_____

Level: First Grade   Name: _____

Small Group Discussions

Directions: When we meet for discussions in First Grade, we contribute to the group by asking questions, listening to others, taking turns, staying on topic, and respecting others' ideas. Use this form during discussions to keep track of how well you participate.

☐ I Take Turns

☐ I Listen To Others

☐ I Stay on Topic

☐ I Respect Others' Ideas

☐ I Ask Questions

Something I learned during today's discussion about _____

was _____

_____

_____

_____

Standard: Reading I Speaking & Listening I SL.1.1   ©http://CoreCommonStandards.com
Graphics (c) ScrappinDoodles

Name: _____

Key Ideas

Directions: Listen to your teacher read a story to the class. Think about the text and write some key ideas that you heard in the text. Draw a picture of one idea. Then, share your paper with the class.

My teacher read a piece of text to us today called:

_____

_____

Here are some key ideas I heard in the text: _____

_____

_____

_____

Here is a picture of one of the ideas I heard in the text.

Level: First Grade   Name: _____

Asking Questions

Directions: Students should ask questions in order to seek help, get information, or clarify something that is not understood. Take anecdotal notes when you hear students asking these kinds of questions.

date:

date:

date:

date:

Name: _____

Telling A Story Orally

Directions: Draw a picture of someone you know, something you do, something you have, or somewhere you have been. Describe your drawing to the class. Use details to express your ideas and feelings.

I can describe something I do, someone I know, something I have, or somewhere I have been.
Here is a picture.

This is a picture of _____

_____

Now, I will share my description with the class.
Here are some words I want to use...

_____

_____

_____

Standard: Reading I Speaking & Listening I SL.1.4   ©http://CoreCommonStandards.com
Graphics (c) ScrappinDoodles

Name: _____

Adding Details

Directions: Give a description and then add detail to the story by drawing a picture.

Describe to a partner a time you were surprised by something or someone.

Add more detail by drawing a picture below.

This is a picture of _____

_____

Tell about what you drew. Use words to describe your ideas, thoughts, and feelings.

Name: _____

Writing Sentences

Directions: Read a story to the class about safety rules. Within a small group, or with partners, students write one or two sentences each that depict the safety rules mentioned in the story to create a poster. Students should write neatly, use proper capitalization and punctuation, and proper verbs and nouns.

Safety Tips

Name: _____

Verbs in Sentences

Directions: Look at the pictures below. Write a sentence for each picture. Use the verbs provided and be sure to use the proper form: IS or ARE.

The ball is rolling.

rolling

The balls are rolling.

rolling

climbing

climbing

cooking

cooking

digging

digging

Standard: Reading I Language I L.1.1

©http://CoreCommonStandards.com

Level: First Grade   Name: _____

Adjectives in Sentences

Directions: Look at the pictures below. Write a sentence for each picture. Use adjectives to describe the pictures. Adjectives describe things like size, color, feelings, shape, and sound.

The worm is happy.

Name: _____

Prepositions in Sentences

Directions: Look at the pictures below. Choose the proper preposition to describe the picture. Write the preposition into the space.

The dog is_____ the leaf.

under   above   behind

Bobby is_____ the box.

during   inside   around

The car drove_____ the tunnel.

above   under   through

Barney is_____ Clyde.

beside   across   between

The tie is_____ her dad.

for   to   from

They walk_____ the bridge.

under   across   outside

Standard: Reading I Language I L.1.1

©http://CoreCommonStandards.com

Name: _____

Fixing Sentences

Directions: Read the sentences below. Correct the words that need capital letters and add the correct punctuation at the end. { . ! ? }

1	larry and stella paint in the park each day
2	let's go to the store with patty
3	why is harold's grocery closed today
4	on thursday we will have meatballs and spaghetti
5	hurry the bus is going to leave soon
6	my dog, scrumples, has a new squeaky toy
7	sowams school has a new principal
8	in february, my school has a valentine's day dance
9	dad brought me to dunkin donuts for a snack
10	does the parkside theatre sell popcorn
11	louisa gave me a CD by the ramones
12	i bought a new shirt at kohl's last saturday

Name: _____

Comma Momma

Directions: Read the sentences below. Insert commas where they belong. Commas are used in dates and to separate words in a series.

1	My birthday is August 9 2006.
2	Mom said I could invite Carrie Penny Violet and Kya.
3	A meteor shower is scheduled for November 18 2012.
4	We will bring pasta meatballs and garlic bread for dinner.
5	At the farm I smell cows pigs horses and hay

Directions: Write a √ for the sentences that are written correctly.

☐ Yesterday, we went to the museum, the zoo, and the playground.

☐ my friend susan had her birthday on august 13 2012

☐ Frank Jane and Floyd are staying at a campground this weekend.

☐ Thursday, November 22, is Thanksgiving Day!

Name: _____

Spelling Words

Directions: Look at the rimes below. Place an onset consonant at the beginning of each word to make new words. You can use single letters or blends. Read the words to a friend.

ock	ear	ight
___ock	___ear	___ight
___ock	___ear	___ight
___ock	___ear	___ight
___ock	___ear	___ight

ate	ool	est
___ate	___ool	___est
___ate	___ool	___est
___ate	___ool	___est
___ate	___ool	___est

Name: _____

Finding Meaning

Directions: Read the sentences below. Look at the underlined word in each sentence. Use the sentence to understand the meaning of the word. Circle the word that means the same as the underlined word.

1. The climber worked his way to the <u>peak</u> of the mountain.

corner	top	base

2. Josie <u>sobbed</u> when she found out her hamster was lost.

cried	laughed	played

3. The clean dishes <u>glistened</u> after mom washed them,

broke	flew	sparkled

4. The monkey at the zoo <u>swung</u> from tree to tree.

sang	moved	ran

5. Little Paulie <u>giggled</u> out loud when his mommy tickled him.

slept	laughed	cried

6. It will take a while for us to <u>ascend</u> the tall hill.

climb	see	buy

Standard: Reading I Language I L.1.4   ©http://CoreCommonStandards.com

Name: _____

Multiple Meanings

Directions: Read the words below. Each word has a sentence that illustrates the word's meaning. Draw a picture for each word to show how it is used in the sentence.

ball I bounce the ball.	**ball** Cinderella went to the ball.
mouse The mouse stole some cheese.	**mouse** I use the mouse on the computer.
bat The bat flew over our heads.	**bat** Casey took the bat and hit the ball.
bark Muffy will bark when the mailman comes.	**bark** There is moss on the tree bark.

Standard: Reading I Language I L.1.4

©http://CoreCommonStandards.com

Name: _____

Multiple Meanings II

Directions: Read the words below. Each word has a sentence that illustrates the word's meaning. Draw a picture for each word to show how it is used in the sentence.

check Mom writes a check to pay the bill.	**check** I always check my work when I am done.
clip I like to help Nana clip coupons.	**clip** Please put the clip back on the chip bag.
club Dad uses a golf club to hit far.	**club** Sally wants to join our new club.
nail Grandpa hit the nail with a hammer.	**nail** I painted each nail a bright red color.

Standard: Reading I Language I L.1.4

©http://CoreCommonStandards.com

Level: First Grade

Name: _____

Categories

Directions: Match the animals to their method of travel. Circle the things the Fly in RED. Circle the things that Walk in BLUE. Circle the things that Swim in GREEN.

Word Attributes

Directions: Read the words below. Think about other words that would describe what the original bold word is. Think about to what categories the word may belong. Write words that are attributes of the original bold word.

Example: <u>**Duck**</u> animal bird swims quacks has feathers lays eggs	<u>**Tree**</u>
<u>**Cake**</u>	<u>**Bicycle**</u>
<u>**Car**</u>	<u>**Crayon**</u>
<u>**Shoe**</u>	<u>**Elephant**</u>

Connecting Words to Life

Directions: Read the words below. Think about things, places, or people in your own life where each word could fit. Write the places, people, or things you think of when you read these words.

Example: Cozy	Delicious
my bed the couch on a rainy day dad's hug	
Frightening	**Exciting**
Loving	**Cuddly**
Smelly	**Wooden**

Name: _____

Conjunction Junction

Directions: Conjunctions can connect sentences. Read the sentences below. Connect and rewrite the sentences using a conjunction. Use: **and, but, or, & because**

My sister bought a new backpack for school.
My brother has to use his old backpack.

_____
_____
_____
_____

Kitty has a new cat toy
Ruff-Ruff has a new dog toy.

_____
_____
_____
_____

Kathy had to go to the dentist.
She had a toothache.

_____
_____
_____
_____

Ryan will have to do his homework when he gets home from school.
He will have to do it in the morning.

_____
_____
_____
_____

Conjunction Junction

Directions: Conjunctions can connect sentences. Read the sentences below. Connect and rewrite the sentences using a conjunction. Use: **however, unless, until, & so**

We had a good time.
It rained.

Mom will make a dessert for the party.
She can think of something else to make.

I was going to sleep over Sarah's.
I didn't feel well.

No one could help me put the boxes in the attic.
I carried them up myself.

Name: _____

In My Own Words

Directions: Read the sentences below. You may have heard the words before. What do you think the words mean? Say or write, in your own words, what you think the words mean.

"After all, a person's a person, no matter how small. "
---*Horton Hears a Who* **by Dr. Seuss**

_____
_____
_____
_____

"But it's no use going back to yesterday, because I was a different person then." --*Alice's Adventures in Wonderland* **by Lewis Caroll**

_____
_____
_____
_____

"There is no comfort in the word 'farewell,' even if you say it in French."
The Tale of Despereaux **by Kate DiCamillo**

_____
_____
_____
_____

"Take chances; make mistakes; get messy!" *The Magic School Bus* **by Joanna Cole**

_____
_____
_____
_____

Common Core
State Standards

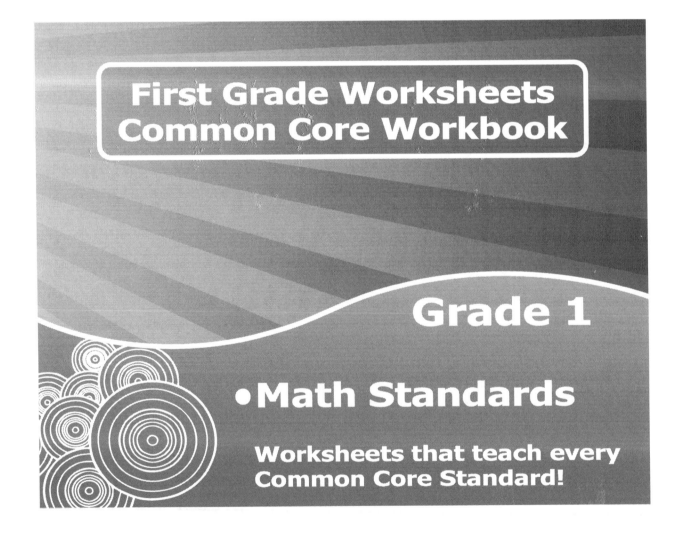

**First Grade Worksheets
Common Core Workbook**

Grade 1

•Math Standards

**Worksheets that teach every
Common Core Standard!**

Addition Word Problems

Directions: Read the addition word problems. Use objects or the spaces below to draw pictures that represent each problem. Then, complete the equation with the correct answer.

5 chickens were in the coop. 8 more chickens flew into the coop. How many chickens were there all together?	7 carrots were picked from the garden on Monday. Jane picked 8 more on Tuesday. How many carrots were picked in all?
5 + 8 = ___	___ + ___ = ___
A box has some kittens inside. Kyle puts 8 into the box. Now there are 19 kittens. How many kittens were in the box at the start?	Susie has 7 jellybeans in her hand. Paul gave her some more, and now she has 20. How many jellybeans did Paul give Susie?
___ + ___ = ___	___ + ___ = ___
Jalisa colored 9 pictures for her mom. Kayla colored 7 pictures for her mom. How many total pictures did the girls color?	Juan scored 8 points in the first half of the game. He scored more in the second half and had a total of 18 points. How many points did Juan score in the second half?
___ + ___ = ___	___ + ___ = ___

Name: _____

Subtraction Word Problems

Directions: Read the subtraction word problems. Use objects or the spaces below to draw pictures that represent each problem. Then, complete the equation with the correct answer.

Laurie brought 15 cupcakes to school. The girls ate 9 of them. The boys ate the rest. How many cupcakes did the boys eat?	Anthony's mom grew 20 flowers in her garden. Anthony picked some. His mom counted only 12 flowers left. How many flowers did Anthony pick?
$$15 - 9 = \_\_\_$$	$$\_\_\_ - \_\_\_ = \_\_\_$$
Kristen watched 14 caterpillars crawling on a leaf. 7 of them went off for a walk. How many caterpillars were left on the leaf?	There were 19 balloons at the birthday party. When the party ended, there were only 6 balloons left. The rest had popped. How many balloons had popped?
$$\_\_\_ - \_\_\_ = \_\_\_$$	$$\_\_\_ - \_\_\_ = \_\_\_$$
Bryan sent out 20 letters to toy stores. He received 13 letters back. How many toy stores did not reply?	Sean built a tower with 17 blocks. The tower fell and only 5 blocks were still standing. How many blocks fell from the tower?
$$\_\_\_ - \_\_\_ = \_\_\_$$	$$\_\_\_ - \_\_\_ = \_\_\_$$

Name: _____

Addition Word Problems

Directions: Read the addition word problems. Use objects or the spaces below to draw pictures that represent each problem. Then, complete the equation with the correct answer.

Margie had 4 red crayons, 6 orange crayons, and 3 blue crayons. How many crayons did Margie have altogether?	In his treasure chest, Brendan had 4 ladybugs, 7 caterpillars, and 1 worm. How many creepy crawlies did Brendan have in all?

$$4 + 6 + 3 = \underline{\quad}$$

$$\underline{\quad} + \underline{\quad} + \underline{\quad} = \underline{\quad}$$

Pam has 2 brothers. Jill has 5 brothers. Linda has 8 brothers. How many brothers do the three girls have in total?	George ran the race in 5 minutes. David ran it in 6 minutes. Larry ran the race in 3 minutes. How many minutes were run altogether?

$$\underline{\quad} + \underline{\quad} + \underline{\quad} = \underline{\quad}$$

$$\underline{\quad} + \underline{\quad} + \underline{\quad} = \underline{\quad}$$

My mom gave me 4 green beans, 8 peas, and 6 pieces of chicken. What was the total amount of food on my plate?	* Ryan had 4 shiny rocks, 6 flat rocks, and some bumpy rocks. He had 15 rocks in all. How many bumpy rocks did Ryan have?

$$\underline{\quad} + \underline{\quad} + \underline{\quad} = \underline{\quad}$$

$$\underline{\quad} + \underline{\quad} + \underline{\quad} = \underline{\quad}$$

Addition Word Problems

Directions: Read the addition word problems. Use objects or the spaces below to draw pictures that represent each problem. Then, complete the equation with the correct answer.

In the last 14 days, it rained 3 days, snowed 6 days, and the rest of the days were sunny. How many days were sunny?

$$3 + 6 + ? = 14$$

Hiram brought 20 bugs to school. He brought 7 beetles, 4 spiders, and some crickets. How many crickets did Hiram bring to school?

__ + __ + __ = ___

The pet store has 18 new pets. They have 5 new dogs, 9 new birds, and some new cats. How many new cats does the pet shop have?

__ + __ + __ = ___

Our chickens lay eggs every day. Monday they laid 4. Tuesday they laid 5. And Wednesday they laid 10. How many eggs did our chickens lay?

__ + __ + __ = ___

At my party I had 3 cousins, 2 best friends, and 8 ballet-class friends. How many kids were at my birthday party?

__ + __ + __ = ___

My nana visited and gave each of us some pennies. She gave me 7 pennies, my sister 5 pennies, and my brother 4 pennies. How many pennies did my Nana bring for us?

__ + __ + __ = ___

Name: _____

I Know This, so I Know...

Directions: Solve the first addition equation. Think about the addends, then solve the second equation. What do you notice?

If I know $4 + 5 =$ ___ then I know that $5 + 4 =$ ___	If I know $3 + 6 =$ ___ then I know that $6 + 3 =$ ___
If I know $7 + 6 =$ ___ then I know that $6 + 7 =$ ___	If I know $8 + 5 =$ ___ then I know that $5 + 8 =$ ___
If I know $2 + 9 =$ ___ then I know that $9 + 2 =$ ___	If I know $8 + 3 =$ ___ then I know that $3 + 8 =$ ___
If I know $9 + 5 =$ ___ then I know that $5 + 9 =$ ___	If I know $7 + 8 =$ ___ then I know that $8 + 7 =$ ___
If I know $10 + 5 =$ ___ then I know that $5 + 10 =$ ___	If I know $6 + 11 =$ ___ then I know that $11 + 6 =$ ___
If I know $12 + 6 =$ ___ then I know that $6 + 12 =$ ___	If I know $8 + 9 =$ ___ then I know that $9 + 8 =$ ___

Standard: Math I Operations & Algebraic Thinking I 1.OA.3   ©www.CoreCommonStandards.com

Find the Ten, Then add...

Directions: Solve the first addition equation. Find the addends that make 10, then rewrite, and solve the second equation.

$4 + 6 + 3 =$ ___ V $10 + 3 = 13$	$3 + 7 + 5 =$ ___ V ___ $+ 5 =$ ___
$4 + 2 + 8 =$ ___ V $4 +$ ___ $=$ ___	$5 + 5 + 9 =$ ___ V ___ $+ 9 =$ ___
$6 + 4 + 2 =$ ___ V ___ $+$ ___ $=$ ___	$2 + 8 + 1 =$ ___ V ___ $+$ ___ $=$ ___
$2 + 1 + 9 =$ ___ V ___ $+$ ___ $=$ ___	$10 + 0 + 6 =$ ___ V ___ $+$ ___ $=$ ___
$7 + 7 + 3 =$ ___ V ___ $+$ ___ $=$ ___	$5 + 5 + 3 =$ ___ V ___ $+$ ___ $=$ ___
★ $2 + 6 + 8 =$ ___ ___ $+$ ___ $=$ ___	★ $3 + 6 + 7 =$ ___ ___ $+$ ___ $=$ ___

Name: _____

Count up to Subtract.

Directions: Solve the first subtraction equation. Use the second equation to help you. Think of it as an addition equation. Count up from one addend to find the unknown addend.

10 - 8 = 2 **find it this way...** **8 + ? = 10**	20 - 5 = 15 find it this way... 5 + ___ = 20
16 - 7 = ___ find it this way... 7 + ___ = 16	18 - 9 = ___ find it this way... 9 + ___ = 18
12 - 10 = ___ find it this way... 10 + ___ = 12	19 - 9 = ___ find it this way... 9 + ___ = 19
17 - 5 = ___ find it this way... 5 + ___ = 17	11 - 6 = ___ find it this way... 6 + ___ = 11
14 - 6 = ___ find it this way... 6 + ___ = 14	10 - 4 = ___ find it this way... 4 + ___ = 10
* 13 - 8 = ___ 8 + ___ = 13	* 15 - 2 = ___ 2 + ___ = 15

Level: First Grade

Name: _____

Fact Families

<u>Directions:</u> Solve the addition and subtraction equations in each house. Do you notice a pattern?

8 + 2 = ____
2 + 8 = ____
10 - 8 = ____
10 - 2 = ____

6 + 7 = ____
7 + 6 = ____
13 - 7 = ____
13 - 6 = ____

9 + 2 = ____
2 + 9 = ____
____ - 9 = ____
____ - 2 = ____

14 + 5 = ____
5 + 14 = ____
____ - 5 = ____
____ - 14 = ____

4 + 8 = ____
8 + 4 = ____
____ - 8 = ____
____ - 4 = ____

9 + 7 = ____
7 + 9 = ____
____ - 9 = ____
____ - 7 = ____

Standard: Math I Operations & Algebraic Thinking I 1.OA.4

©www.CoreCommonStandards.com

94

Counting On to Add

Directions: Count on from one number to another number to solve the addition equations.

I can count on 5 from 10... 10... **11, 12, 13, 14, 15** **10 + 5 = 15**	I can count on 4 from 12... 12... **13, 14, 15, 16** **12 + 4 = ___**
I can count on 7 from 11... 11... ___, ___, ___, ___, ___, ___, ___ **11 + 7 = ___**	I can count on 8 from 10... 10... ___, ___, ___, ___, ___, ___, ___, ___ **10 + 8 = ___**
I can count on 9 from 9... 9... ___, ___, ___, ___, ___, ___, ___, ___, ___ **9 + 9 = ___**	I can count on 3 from 17... 17... ___, ___, ___ **17 + 3 = ___**
I can count on 5 from 13... 13... ___, ___, ___, ___, ___ **13 + 5 = ___**	I can count on 10 from 7... 7... ___, ___, ___, ___, ___, ___, ___, ___, ___, ___ **7 + 10 = ___**

Name: _____

Counting Back to Subtract

<u>Directions:</u> Count back from one number to another number to solve the subtraction equations.

I can count back 5 from 15... 15... **14, 13, 12, 11, 10** $15 - 5 = 10$	I can count back 6 from 18... 18... **17, 16, 15, 14, 13, 12,** $18 - 6 = $ ___
I can count back 7 from 18... 18... ___, ___, ___, ___, ___, ___, ___ $18 - 7 = $ ___	I can count back 4 from 20... 20... ___, ___, ___, ___ $20 - 4 = $ ___
I can count back 8 from 16... 16... ___, ___, ___, ___, ___, ___, ___, ___ $16 - 8 = $ ___	I can count back 5 from 17... 17... ___, ___, ___, ___, ___ $17 - 5 = $ ___
I can count back 10 from 20... 20... ___, ___, ___, ___, ___, ___, ___, ___, ___, ___ $20 - 10 = $ ___	I can count back 9 from 16... 16... ___, ___, ___, ___, ___, ___, ___, ___, ___ $16 - 9 = $ ___

Name: _____

Ways to Find the Number

<u>Directions:</u> Solve the addition equations. Use strategies you have learned to solve the problems...*Counting Up, Finding a Ten, Breaking it Down.* Show your thinking.

$14 + 3 = $ ___ *14...15, 16, 17* *14 + 3 = 17*	$8 + 6 = $ ___ V *4 + **4 + 6** = * ___ V **4 + 10 = 14**
1. $4 + 5 + 5 = $ ___	**2.** $12 + 8 + 3 = $ ___
3. $17 + 5 = $ ___	**4.** $8 + 9 = $ ___
5. $2 + 5 + 8 = $ ___	**6.** $3 + 10 = $ ___
7. $7 + 12 + 1 = $ ___	**8.** $15 + 6 = $ ___

Standard: Math I Operations & Algebraic Thinking I 1.OA.6   ©www.CoreCommonStandards.com

Name: _____

Ways to Find the Number

<u>Directions:</u> Solve the subtraction equations. Use strategies you have learned to solve the problems...*Counting Down, Finding a Ten, Breaking it Down.* Show your thinking.

$15 - 7 = $ ___ *15...14, 13, 12, 11, 10, 9, 8* *15 - 7 = 8*	$13 - 4 = $ ___ V $13 - 3 - 1 = $ ___ V **10 - 1** $= 9$
(1.) $19 - 7 = $ ___	(2.) $15 - 8 = $ ___
(3.) $14 - 5 = $ ___	(4.) $20 - 8 = $ ___
(5.) $18 - 4 = $ ___	(6.) $17 - 12 = $ ___
(7.) $13 - 8 = $ ___	(8.) $19 - 10 = $ ___

Standard: Math I Operations & Algebraic Thinking I 1.OA.6   ©www.CoreCommonStandards.com

Name: _____

True or False?

<u>Directions:</u> Read the addition equations below. Are they true? Are both sides of the equal sign the same? Fill in the bubbles that show the true equations.

Sample 2 + 4 = 4 + 2 B 4 + 3 = 4 + 4	1. A 5 + 3 + 1 = 4 + 5 B 4 + 4 + 2 = 8 + 1 + 2
2. A 5 + 5 = 2 + 2 + 3 B 3 + 1 = 2 + 2	3. A 2 + 6 = 4 + 5 B 6 + 4 + 1 = 7 + 1 + 3
4. A 3 + 3 + 3 = 4 + 4 B 3 + 3 + 3 = 4 + 4	5. A 8 + 5 = 10 + 3 B 12 + 5 = 10 + 3
6. A 9 + 3 = 3 + 9 B 9 + 12 = 8 + 4	7. A 3 + 4 = 5 + 2 B 9 + 3 = 11 + 2
8. A 8 + 4 = 2 + 5 B 17 + 5 = 5 + 17	9. A 2 + 7 = 8 + 1 B 12 + 4 = 2 + 4

Level: First Grade

Name: _____

True or False?

<u>Directions:</u> Read the subtraction equations below. Are they true? Are both sides of the equal sign the same? Fill in the bubbles that show the true equations.

Sample	A	5 - 5 = 4 - 4
	B	4 - 3 = 4 - 4

1.	A	8 - 3 = 3 - 2
	B	9 - 3 = 8 - 2

2.	A	6 - 2 = 8 - 4
	B	4 - 1 = 9 - 2

3.	A	6 - 3 = 3 - 3
	B	6 - 1 = 9 - 4

4.	A	12 - 3 = 10 - 1
	B	8 - 4 = 5 - 3

5.	A	13 - 3 = 15 - 5
	B	13 - 0 = 15 - 0

6.	A	5 - 4 = 6 - 5
	B	12 - 6 = 6 - 3

7.	A	7 - 3 = 5 - 2
	B	9 - 3 = 6 - 0

8.	A	8 - 4 = 2 - 1
	B	10 - 5 = 5 - 0

9.	A	7 - 2 = 10 - 5
	B	12 - 2 = 10 - 1

Level: First Grade   Name: _____

True or False?

<u>Directions:</u> Read the equations below. Are they true? Are both sides of the equal sign the same? Fill in the bubbles that show the true equations.

Sample **A** $3 + 4 = 4 + 3$ **B** $7 + 1 = 4 + 4$ Ⓒ $5 + 1 = 7 + 2$	**1.** Ⓐ $2 + 3 + 4 = 4 + 5$ Ⓑ $8 + 10 + 2 = 5 + 1 + 6$ Ⓒ $9 + 3 + 1 = 7 + 3 + 3$	
2. Ⓐ $8 + 1 = 3 + 3 + 3$ Ⓑ $5 + 1 = 7 + 0$ Ⓒ $5 + 1 + 2 = 8 + 0$	**3.** Ⓐ $8 + 1 = 4 + 5$ Ⓑ $3 + 2 + 9 = 7 + 1 + 5$ Ⓒ $4 + 4 = 2 + 3$	
4. Ⓐ $9 + 1 + 6 = 7 + 3 + 2$ Ⓑ $5 + 2 + 10 = 8 + 3 + 3$ Ⓒ $9 + 2 + 8 = 10 + 10 + 2$	**5.** Ⓐ $8 - 5 = 10 - 2$ Ⓑ $12 - 5 = 10 - 3$ Ⓒ $12 - 5 = 13 - 2$	
6. Ⓐ $9 - 3 = 10 - 4$ Ⓑ $17 - 12 = 19 - 4$ Ⓒ $16 - 10 = 8 - 2$	**7.** Ⓐ $20 - 14 = 18 - 12$ Ⓑ $18 - 3 = 14 - 4$ Ⓒ $15 - 4 = 19 - 8$	
8. Ⓐ $18 - 14 = 20 - 15$ Ⓑ $17 - 5 = 14 - 9$ Ⓒ $12 - 5 = 15 - 3$	**9.** Ⓐ $20 - 7 = 20 - 6$ Ⓑ $14 - 6 = 19 - 11$ Ⓒ $18 - 4 = 14 - 2$	

True or False?

<u>Directions:</u> Read the equations below. Are they true? Are both sides of the equal sign the same? Fill in the bubbles that show the true equations.

Sample		1.	
A $4 + 2 + 5 = 8 + 2 + 1$		Ⓐ $4 + 1 + 5 = 19 - 4$	
B $7 + 3 = 15 - 5$		Ⓑ $16 - 8 = 4 + 2 + 2$	
C $12 - 9 = 5 - 2$		Ⓒ $17 - 5 = 12 - 0$	

2.		3.	
Ⓐ $16 + 0 = 13 + 3$		Ⓐ $5 + 6 + 4 = 20 - 5$	
Ⓑ $19 - 5 = 7 + 7$		Ⓑ $7 + 12 = 13 + 6$	
Ⓒ $6 + 3 = 20 - 11$		Ⓒ $17 - 6 = 14 - 3$	

4.		5.	
Ⓐ $9 + 1 + 3 = 6 + 3 + 1$		Ⓐ $18 - 5 = 10 + 3$	
Ⓑ $5 + 1 + 10 = 18 - 2$		Ⓑ $12 - 5 = 5 + 2$	
Ⓒ $2 + 4 + 12 = 20 - 0$		Ⓒ $10 + 3 + 2 = 17 - 6$	

6.		7.	
Ⓐ $19 - 5 = 7 + 7$		Ⓐ $12 + 5 = 10 + 7$	
Ⓑ $18 + 1 = 13 + 5$		Ⓑ $16 - 8 = 4 + 4$	
Ⓒ $15 - 7 = 5 + 3$		Ⓒ $3 + 9 + 1 = 20 - 7$	

8.		9.	
Ⓐ $14 + 3 = 20 - 3$		Ⓐ $12 - 0 = 7 + 2$	
Ⓑ $4 + 4 + 4 = 10 + 2$		Ⓑ $6 + 12 = 14 + 4$	
Ⓒ $5 + 3 = 19 - 5$		Ⓒ $20 - 8 = 10 + 2$	

Name: _____

Make it True

Directions: Read the equations below. What missing number makes the equations true? Write the missing numbers into the equations.

$5 + 6 =$ ___	___ $+ 7 = 10$
$12 -$ ___ $= 8$	$16 - 8 =$ ___
___ $+ 5 = 19$	$12 + 6 =$ ___
$13 -$ ___ $= 9$	$20 - 7 =$ ___
___ $- 5 = 15$	$19 +$ ___ $= 20$
$14 -$ ___ $= 7$	___ $+ 13 = 17$
$9 + 2 + 9 =$ ___	___ $- 7 = 10$
$2 +$ ___ $+ 5 = 18$	$10 + 4 +$ ___ $= 19$

Name: _____

Make it True

Directions: Read the equations below. What missing number makes the equations true? Write the missing numbers into the equations.

$3 + 2 + 1 = 9 - \underline{}$	$20 - 7 = 9 + \underline{} + 1$
$11 + \underline{} = 4 + 1 + 10$	$19 - 1 = 10 + \underline{}$
$15 + 3 = 20 - \underline{}$	$16 - \underline{} = 4 + 4$
$\underline{} + 5 = 13 + 6$	$12 - 4 = 16 - \underline{}$
$20 - 4 = \underline{} + 5$	$11 + 7 = 6 + 3 + \underline{}$
$10 + 2 + 2 = 17 - \underline{}$	$16 - 8 = 9 - \underline{}$
$1 + 19 = 20 - \underline{}$	$14 + 2 = 19 - \underline{}$
$18 - 7 = 13 - \underline{}$	$2 + 8 + \underline{} = 7 + 6$

Name: _____

I Can Count to One Hundred Twenty!

Directions: Start at 0 and count to 120 by **ONES** and **TENS**.

0	1	2	3	4	5	6	7	8	9
10	11	12	13	14	15	16	17	18	19
20	21	22	23	24	25	26	27	28	29
30	31	32	33	34	35	36	37	38	39
40	41	42	43	44	45	46	47	48	49
50	51	52	53	54	55	56	57	58	59
60	61	62	63	64	65	66	67	68	69
70	71	72	73	74	75	76	77	78	79
80	81	82	83	84	85	86	87	88	89
90	91	92	93	94	95	96	97	98	99
100	101	102	103	104	105	106	107	108	109
110	111	112	113	114	115	116	117	118	119
120									

Standard: Math | Number & Operations in Base Ten | 1.NBT.1

Name: _____

I Can Write Numbers to One Hundred Twenty!

Directions: Start at 0 and count to 120. Write the numbers that are missing from the chart.

0	1	2	3	4	5	6	7	8	9
10							17		
				24					
			33			36			
		42							
	51								
				65					
70									
									89
								98	
100				104					
	111				115				
120									

Standard: Math I Number & Operations in Base Ten I 1.NBT.1

©www.CoreCommonStandards.com

Name: _____

Counting Tens and Ones

Directions: Count the tens and ones below. Write how many tens and ones there are in the chart. Then write the number the 2 digits create.

1.

tens	ones

_____

2.

tens	ones

_____

3.

tens	ones

_____

4.

tens	ones

_____

5.

tens	ones

_____

6.

tens	ones

_____

7.

tens	ones

_____

8.

tens	ones

_____

Standard: Math I Number & Operations in Base Ten I 1.NBT.2   ©www.CoreCommonStandards.com

Drawing Tens and Ones

<u>Directions:</u> Look at the number in each box. Draw tens and ones to represent the number. You can use objects to help you. Try to write an equation for each number.

<u>48</u> 40 + 8 = 48	<u>37</u>
<u>59</u>	<u>26</u>
<u>19</u>	<u>73</u>
<u>68</u>	<u>84</u>

Name: _____

Comparing Tens and Ones

Directions: Compare the two-digit numbers. Think about tens and ones.

Write in <, =, or > to make the equation true.

<   =   >

17 __ 19	57 __ 15	31 __ 74	31 __ 38
22 __ 23	65 __ 56	13 __ 73	17 __ 71
85 __ 28	73 __ 37	41 __ 49	63 __ 93
24 __ 52	63 __ 63	83 __ 90	47 __ 27
51 __ 41	68 __ 64	10 __ 50	19 __ 19
99 __ 49	56 __ 65	27 __ 27	39 __ 89
62 __ 62	33 __ 63	79 __ 69	22 __ 27
93 __ 95	69 __ 45	65 __ 55	16 __ 13

Name: _____

Greater and Less and In Between

Directions: Read the sentences. Write a number that is between the two given numbers in each sentence.

Write a number that is greater than 45 and less than 60.	_____
Write a number that is greater than 27 and less than 39.	_____
Write a number that is greater than 80 and less than 93.	_____
Write a number that is greater than 16 and less than 28.	_____
Write a number that is greater than 77 and less than 87.	_____
Write a number that is greater than 61 and less than 93.	_____
Write a number that is greater than 34 and less than 43.	_____
Write a number that is greater than 88 and less than 92.	_____
Write a number that is greater than 32 and less than 45.	_____

Name: _____

Adding Tens and Ones

Directions: Add the tens and ones below. (No regrouping)

10	15	40	50
+ 30	+30	+17	+20

20	60	65	29
+45	+ 7	+ 3	+40

30 + 34 = [ ]   50 + 41 = [ ]

37 + 20 = [ ]   32 + 6 = [ ]

30 + 12 = [ ]   50 + 39 = [ ]

40 + 4 = [ ]   36 + 10 = [ ]

Name: _____

Adding Tens and Ones

<u>Directions:</u> Add the tens and ones below. (Some regrouping)

40	35	20	11
+ 67	+49	+68	+48

50	36	47	30
+36	+ 7	+ 5	+59

29 + 48 = ☐   52 + 31 = ☐

28 + 30 = ☐   71 + 6 = ☐

17 + 33 = ☐   54 + 9 = ☐

35 + 44 = ☐   34 + 29 = ☐

Name: _____

Ten Less, Ten More

Directions: Look at the grids below. Write the numbers that are ten less and ten more than the numbers shown. (Think about the Hundreds Grid.)

1.
—
25
—

2.
—
37
—

3.
—
46
—

4.
—
79
—

5.
—
81
—

6.
—
68
—

7.
—
16
—

8.
—
53
—

9.
—
90
—

Ten More and Ten Less

Directions: Look at the numbers below. Think about the tens and ones. Write the number ten less or ten more than the numbers shown.

34 _____	46 _____
_____ 72	_____ 56
81 _____	39 _____
_____ 17	_____ 20
55 _____	84 _____
_____ 63	_____ 19
48 _____	25 _____
_____ 87	_____ 93

Name: _____

Subtracting Tens and Ones

<u>Directions:</u> Subtract the tens and ones below.

30	40	80	50
- 20	- 30	- 40	- 20

60	30	90	70
- 20	- 10	- 50	- 20

70 - 30 = [ ]   50 - 40 = [ ]

40 - 20 = [ ]   70 - 60 = [ ]

30 - 30 = [ ]   50 - 10 = [ ]

80 - 50 = [ ]   60 - 30 = [ ]

Name: _____

Subtracting Tens and Ones

<u>Directions:</u> Subtract the tens and ones below.

46	58	32	61
- 10	- 30	- 20	- 40

84	97	75	83
- 60	- 50	- 50	- 40

Show your thinking below by using drawings, words, or the number line.

Level: First Grade   Name: _____

Ordering Objects

<u>Directions:</u> Look at the pictures below. Look at their lengths. Write 1, 2, and 3 in the spaces to show the order of the objects from shortest to longest.

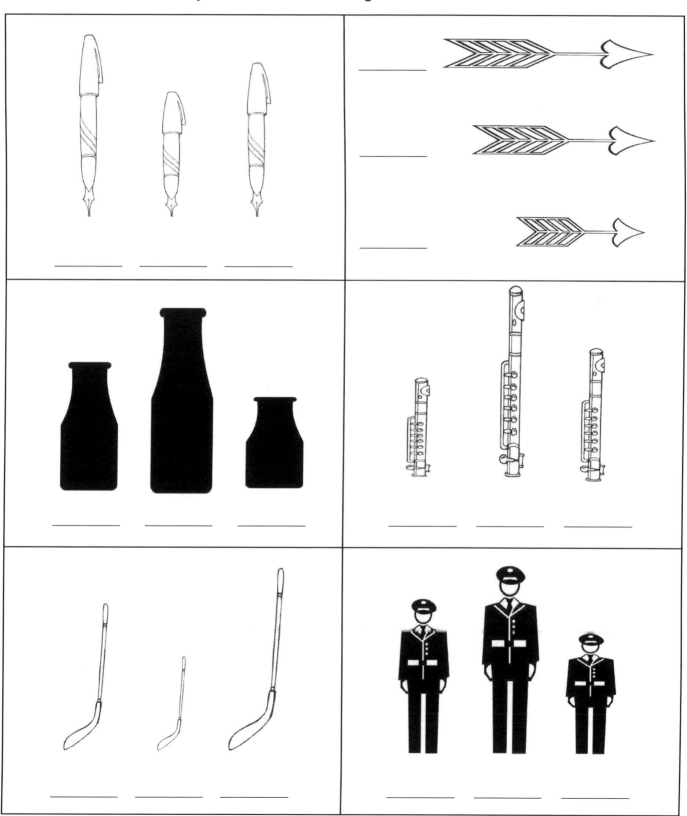

Standard: Math I Operations & Algebraic Thinking I 1.MD.1   ©www.CoreCommonStandards.com

Level: First Grade   Name: _____

Ordering Objects

Directions: Look at the pictures below. Look at their lengths. Write 1, 2, and 3 in the spaces to show the order of the objects from shortest to longest.

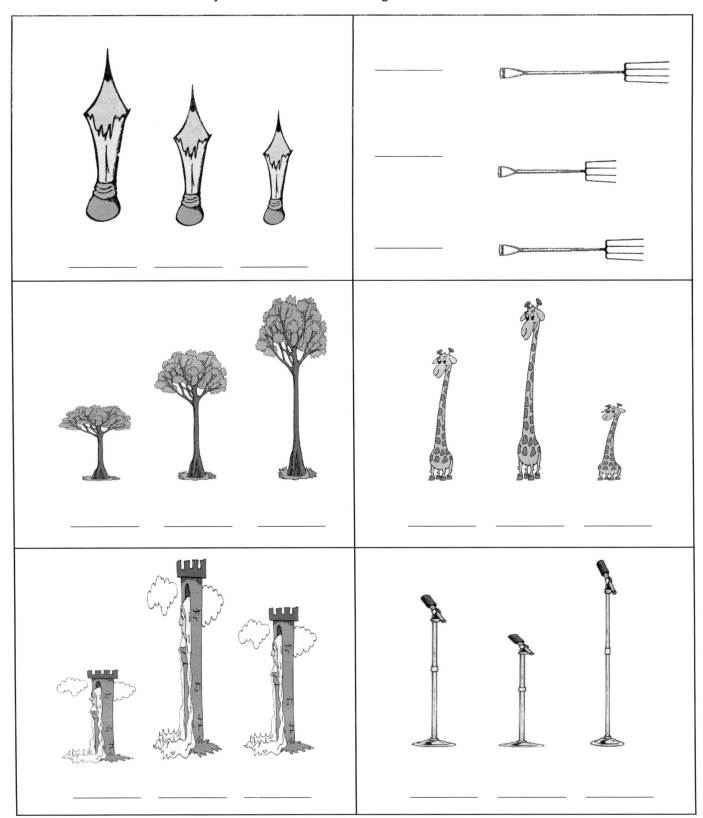

Name: _____

Measuring Objects

Directions: Measure the objects below by counting the units. Write the total number of units for each object.

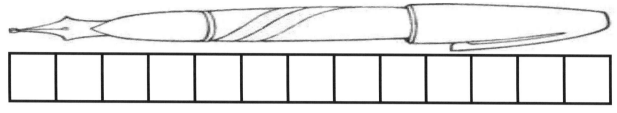

The pen is _____ units long.

The rod is _____ units long.

The spoon is _____ units long.

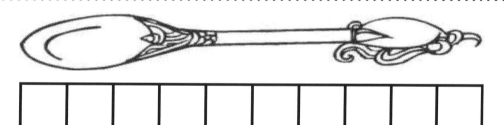

The tube is _____ units long.

Standard: Math | Operations & Algebraic Thinking | 1.MD.2   ©www.CoreCommonStandards.com

Name: _____

Measuring Objects

<u>Directions:</u> Measure the objects below by counting the units. Write the total number of units for each object.

The bat is _____ units long.

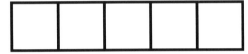

The chisel is _____ units long.

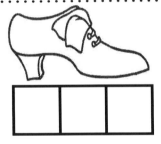

The shoe is _____ units long.

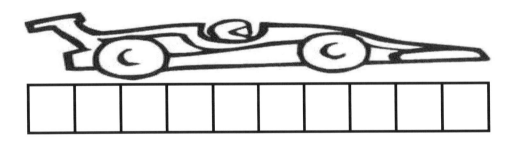

The car is _____ units long.

Level: First Grade

Name: _____

What Time is It?

Directions: Look at the clocks below. What time is it? Write the digital times beneath the clocks.

___:___	___:___	___:___
___:___	___:___	___:___
___:___	___:___	___:___
___:___	___:___	___:___

Standard: Math I Measurement & Data I 1.MD.3

©www.CoreCommonStandards.com

Name: _____

What Time is It?

Directions: Look at the clocks below. Draw the hands correctly to show the digital time below each clock.   Hour ———➤   Minute ———➤

4:00	5:30	6:00
11:30	10:00	9:30
12:30	9:00	12:00
1:30	2:00	7:30

Name: _____

Balloons

<u>Directions:</u> Using the data in the graph below, answer the questions about balloons.

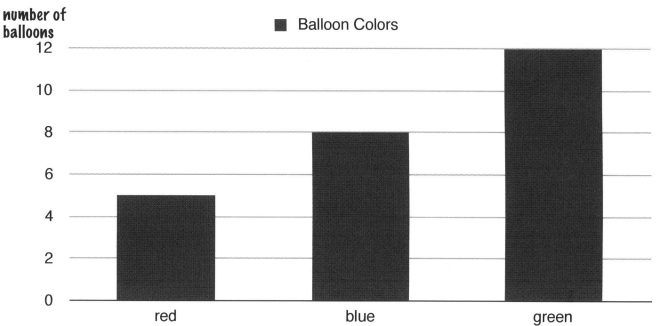

Kara blew up some balloons for the party. Answer the questions about her balloons using the graph above.

1. How many red balloons does Kara have?

_____

2. How many green balloons does Kara have?

_____

3. How many more blue balloons are there than red balloons?

_____

4. How many balloons are there altogether?

_____

5. What was the total amount of green and red balloons?

_____

Name: _____

Make a Graph Using Data

<u>Directions:</u> Read the problem below. Create a graph that will represent the data. Ask 3 questions that can be answered by using the graph. Write the answers. Don't forget to label.

Wanda brought 19 cupcakes to her classroom for a snack. She had three different flavors. Create a graph that shows the flavors and how many of each there could be.

Write three questions that can be answered using your graph. Answer the questions.

_____

_____

_____

_____

_____

_____

_____

Level: First Grade

Name: _____

Triangles, Rectangles, Or Not?

Directions: Look at the shapes below. Think about the attributes of triangles and rectangles. Circle the triangles RED, Circle the rectangles BLUE.

Standard: Math I Geometry I 1.G.1

©www.CoreCommonStandards.com

Name: _____

Drawing By the Rules

Directions: Think about the attributes of 2-D shapes. Draw the shapes listed below. Write a few words that explain the attributes of each shape. (Some words you may use...line, angle, closed, curve, number)

Circle	Square	Rectangle
_____	_____	_____
_____	_____	_____
Triangle	**Hexagon**	**Pentagon**
_____	_____	_____
_____	_____	_____

©www.CoreCommonStandards.com

Level: First Grade   Name: _____

Making Composite Shapes

Directions: Using straws and twist ties, or other building materials, construct 2-D shapes and 3-D shapes to create composite shapes. Draw some of the shapes you created. Label the shapes that created the composite shape.

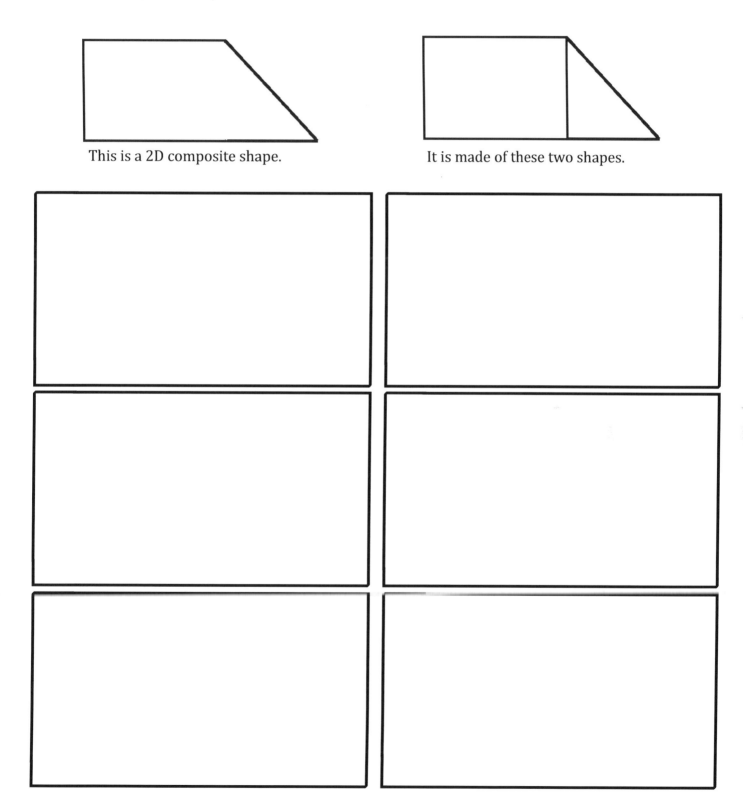

This is a 2D composite shape.   It is made of these two shapes.

Name: _____

Making Composite Shapes

Directions: Look at the composite shapes below. What smaller shapes do you see? Draw lines to show other smaller shapes within the larger shapes.

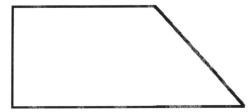

This is a 2D composite shape.

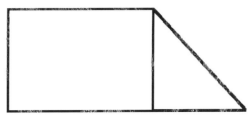

It is made of these two shapes.

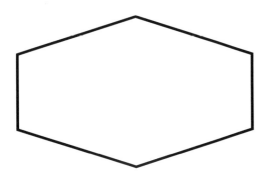

I see _____

_____

_____

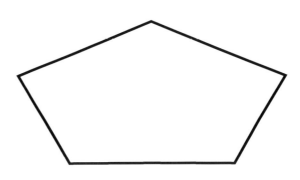

I see _____

_____

_____

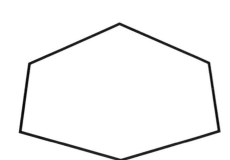

I see _____

_____

_____

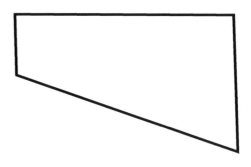

I see _____

_____

_____

Standard: Math | Geometry | 1.G.2

©www.CoreCommonStandards.com

Halves and Fourths

Directions: Shade in the proper amount.

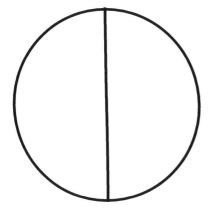

This circle is split into 2 equal parts called *halves*.

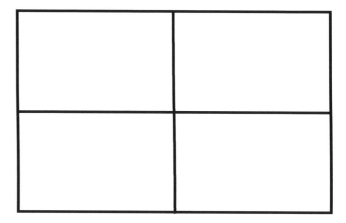

This rectangle is split into 4 equal parts called fourths, or quarters.

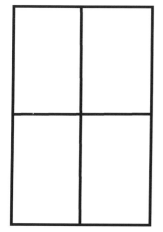

Shade one fourth.

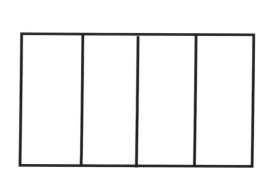

Shade one fourth.

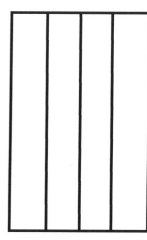

Shade one fourth.

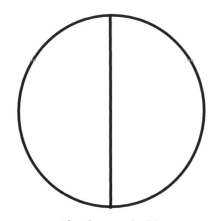

Shade one half.

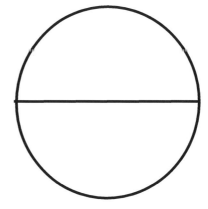

Shade one half.

Name: _____

Halves and Fourths

Directions: Draw lines and shade in the proper amount.

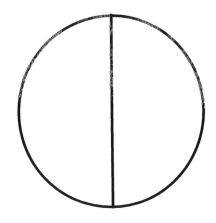

This circle is split into 2 equal parts called *halves*.

This rectangle is split into 4 equal parts called fourths, or quarters.

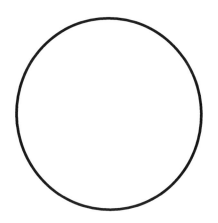

Shade one half.

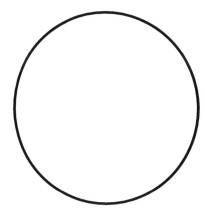

Shade two halves.

Shade one fourth.

Shade two fourths.

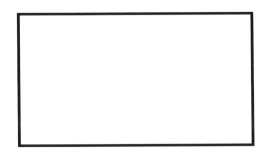

Shade three fourths.

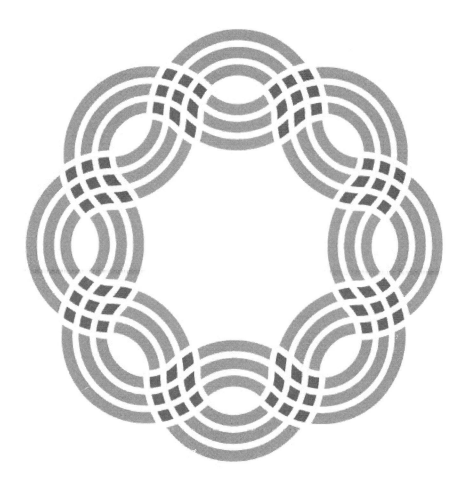

Made in the USA
San Bernardino, CA
30 January 2016